STONE OFFERINGS

STONE OFFERINGS

Machu Picchu's Terraces of Enlightenment

MIKE TORREY

Introduction by Marie Arana

Spanish Translation by Isabel Arana Cisneros

LIGHTPOINT PRESS

Published by
Lightpoint Press
4079 Governor Drive, Suite 272
San Diego, CA 92122
info@stoneofferings.com
www.stoneofferings.com

Publisher's Cataloging-in-Publication Data
Torrey, Mike. Stone Offerings: Machu Picchu's Terraces of Enlightenment / MikeTorrey;
Introduction by Marie Arana; Spanish Translations by Isabel Arana Cisneros. —San Diego, CA: Lightpoint Press, ©2009.
p.; cm.
ISBN-13: 978-0-9818812-0-1
ISBN-10: 0-9818812-0-3
Includes index.
1. Machu Picchu Site (Peru)—Pictorial works. 2. Inca architecture—Pictorial works.
I. Arana, Marie. II. Title. III. Title:Machu Picchu's Terraces of Enlightenment.
F3429.1.M3 T67 2009   2008933585
985.37—dc22   0906

Produced and edited by Karla Olson, BookStudio, LLC
Photoediting by Kirsten Rian
Interior and jacket design by Claudine Mansour Design

Printed by Everbest Printing Company Ltd., China
Distributed by SCB Distributors

First Edition
10 9 8 7 6 5 4 3 2 1

OFFERINGS REMEMBERED

for my father and grandmother

INTRODUCTION

INTRODUCCIÓN

We humans long to touch the sky. We may be tied to Earth but, as the Inca knew, we seek the sun. We sail the seas, reckoning by stars. We mark our seasons by the moon. We scale tall mountains to reach high ground. We bless those promontories as sacred places. We call them the abodes of gods. Nowhere is this impulse more evident than in the vertiginous heights of the Andean cordillera where, more than five hundred years ago, the Inca pierced the heavens with a mighty citadel of stone. "Ancient Peak," they called it. Machu Picchu.

Vacant for more than four centuries, this towering fortress survived to become one of the world's great enigmas. After the conquistadors sacked the Inca, after they infected America with a virulent plague of small pox, Machu Picchu was reduced to a hull of its former splendor, overrun by a tropical forest that crept up to lock it in time's embrace. Except for a handful of farmers who planted its lofty terraces, few knew it existed. The site was erased from history. Lost to civilization. Suspended in mist.

Legend has it that it was built in the 1450s by the Inca emperor Pachacutec, whose very name means "he who transforms the world." Remake the empire is precisely what Pachacutec did. He conquered the Chanca, a fierce people whose territorial ambitions and bloodlust had tormented the Inca for generations. He built a mighty federation, which he called the Tawantinsuyu—literally "four corners of the earth"—a dominion that spread from Cusco to nearly the whole of civilized South America.

Once Pachacutec's engineers were finished restoring the capital of Cusco, it is said they were charged with constructing

Nosotros los seres humanos anhelamos tocar con nuestras manos el cielo. Podemos estar atados a la tierra, pero, como lo supo el Inca, buscamos el Sol. Navegamos en los mares guiados por las estrellas. La luna marca nuestras estaciones. Subimos a montañas muy altas para situarnos en tierras elevadas. Bendecimos aquellos promontorios como si fueran lugares sagrados. Los llamamos moradas de los dioses. En ninguna parte es este impulso más evidente que en las alturas vertiginosas de la cordillera de los Andes, donde hace más de quinientos años, el Inca perforó los cielos con una poderosa ciudadela de piedra. "Pico Antiguo" le llamaron. Machu Picchu.

Inhabitada por más de cuatro centurias, esta dominante fortaleza sobrevivió para convertirse en uno de los más grandes enigmas del mundo. Después de que los Conquistadores saquearon los dominios del Inca, después de que ellos infectaron América con la plaga virulenta que fue la viruela, Machu Picchu se redujo a convertirse en tan sólo la corteza de lo que fue su antiguo esplendor, invadida por una selva tropical que se encaramó sobre ella, para encarcelarla dentro del abrazo del tiempo. Con excepción de un puñado de agricultores que sembraron sus altos andenes, pocos seres supieron de su existencia. El lugar fue borrado de la historia. Perdido para la civilización. Suspendido en la niebla.

Cuenta la leyenda que la fortaleza fue construida cerca del año 1450, por el emperador Pachacútec, cuyo nombre significa realmente "Aquel que transforma el mundo". Lo que Pachacútec hizo fue precisamente rehacer el imperio. Conquistó a los Chancas, pueblo fiero, cuyas ambiciones territoriales, y cuya sed de sangre habían atormentado al Inca durante generaciones. El construyó una confederación poderosa a la cual llamó El Tawantinsuyo—literalmente "Las cuatro esquinas del

an impenetrable refuge for the Inca aristocracy. They chose a mountain aerie fifty miles northwest of Cusco, a fertile saddle of green perched more than a mile and a half above sea level and two thousand feet over the Urubamba River. With plunging escarpments on either side, Machu Picchu was virtually unreachable except for a closely guarded path that led to a single stone door. But Pachacutec's engineers had noted something more about this magical landform. It was the way the sun aligned on its zenith; the way stars moved overhead. Its sheer height. The thin air. The unmistakable feeling that came over them when they stood on that peak, half trammeled to rock, half soaring in sky.

As little as we know about Machu Picchu, we know less about how the Inca built it. They had to haul ten-ton boulders up precipitous cliffs with no beasts of burden. They had to cut and polish those massive stones without iron tools. They had to fit them together with no bond or mortar. That Machu Picchu still stands is a tribute to their craft and ingenuity, for there is no question that the site is a superhuman feat of architectural planning, a marvel of scientific acuity—a veritable wonder of the world.

I often say that I, like the mighty Inca, spent years imagining Machu Picchu. By the time I was a small girl growing up on the Peruvian coast, that mountain sanctuary had reached mythical proportions in my impressionable mind. I was told it had been "discovered" by the American professor Hiram Bingham a mere generation before me; that the mystery it posed to the world was profound and unsolvable. What was it meant to be, a retreat or a temple? Who were its builders, warriors or priests? My brother and I, a mere seven and six at the time, set out to dig the earth around our family house, sure that it would surrender similar treasures. We knew the names of the Inca emperors by heart. We knew that the ground held their secrets. Perhaps we, too, could wrest history from the dust.

mundo"—un dominio que se extendió desde Cusco hasta el total de las regiones civilizadas de Sudamérica.

Cuando los ingenieros de Pachacútec terminaron de restaurar la capital de Cusco, se dice que fueron encargados de construir un refugio impenetrable para la aristocracia que rodeaba al Inca. Escogieron una montaña alta cual refugio de águilas, cincuenta millas al noroeste de Cusco, un prado fértil y florido, a más de una milla y media sobre el nivel del mar, y a dos mil piés sobre el río Urubamba. Con rocas escarpadas sumergidas por todos lados, Machu Picchu era virtualmente inalcanzable, con excepción de un sendero cuidadosamente defendido que conducía a una pequeña puerta labrada en piedra. Pero los ingenieros de Pachacútec habían advertido algo más acerca de estos lugares mágicos, y era el modo como se alineaba el Sol sobre su cenit y la manera como se desplazaban las estrellas en el cielo. Su altura transparente. El aire tenue. El indudable sentimiento que les invadía cuando se erguían sobre ese pico. Se sentían amarrados a las piedras y, al mismo tiempo, elevados hacia las alturas.

Sabemos poco acerca de Machu Picchu, menos aún de cómo lo construyó el Inca. Tuvieron que arrastrar enormes piedras hacia precipicios de acantilados, sin ayuda de bestias de carga. Tuvieron que cortar y pulir estas piedras gigantescas sin tener herramientas de hierro. Tuvieron que acomodarlas y unirlas sin ninguna mezcla ni mortero. Que Machu Picchu todavía permanezca igual es un tributo a su habilidad y a su inventiva. No hay duda de que el lugar representa una hazaña sobrehumana de planeamiento arquitectónico, un prodigio de agudeza científica—una verdadera maravilla del mundo.

Yo digo a menudo que yo, como el poderoso Inca empleé muchos años imaginando Machu Picchu. En la época en que yo era una niña pequeña que crecía en la costa peruana, esa montaña y su santuario habían alcanzado proporciones míticas en mi mente impresionable. Se me dijo que la fortaleza había sido "descubierta" por el profesor norteamericano Hiram Bingham, hacía muy poco tiempo, solamente en

What we didn't understand was how complicated that history had been. Much of Machu Picchu was gone by the time the larger world heard of it. And, since the Inca had no written language, it wasn't until the sixteenth century that it was described. The Peruvian chronicler El Inca Garcilaso de la Vega wrote that the famed Temple of the Sun had once been laminated in gold and encrusted with gemstones. The one hundred tombs that lay beneath the terraces had held sacrificial mummies, intricate textiles, and precious relics. But by the time the *National Geographic* magazine published its famous April 1913 issue dedicated entirely to Bingham's find, the site was essentially what we see today—long, enigmatic walls of stone, serpentine terraces, puzzling structures with trapezoidal doors and windows, polished ceremonial rock.

In truth, Bingham had not been the first to stumble on Machu Picchu after the Inca abandoned it. It seems that in the late 1800s, Augusto Berns, a German adventurer, scaled the mountain and looted the citadel's gold. Historians now claim that he probably spirited thousands of objects to Europe and sold them to universities and museums, where pre-Columbian artifacts began to appear in unprecedented quantities. There is plenty of evidence, too, that indigenous scholars and residents of Cusco were well aware of Machu Picchu before Bingham located it. But it was not until 1911, when one of them scouted the trail for the Yale University lecturer, that the place gained its world renown. Within a few years, Bingham had transported more than five thousand relics from Machu Picchu to the Peabody Museum at Yale. More than ninety years later, in 2007, the university began negotiations to return them.

Not that any of this will matter to the pilgrim who climbs her dizzying way to Machu Picchu. Despite its fraught history, despite its essential mysteries, the place still exudes a timeless

una generación anterior a la mía; que el misterio que mostraba ante el mundo era profundo y sin solución. ¿Qué se suponía que era—un refugio o un templo? ¿Quiénes fueron sus constructores—guerreros o sacerdotes? Mi hermano y yo, unos pequeños niños de siete y seis años en ese tiempo, nos pusimos a cavar la tierra alrededor de nuestra casa, seguros de que nos podrían proporcionar tesoros parecidos. Sabíamos de memoria los nombres de los emperadores incaicos. Sabíamos que el suelo poseía secretos. Tal vez nosotros también podríamos arrancar del polvo algo de su historia.

Lo que nosotros no comprendimos fue lo complicada que había sido esa historia. Mucho de lo que rodeaba a Machu Picchu había desaparecido en la época en que el extenso mundo se enteró de su existencia. Y, como los Incas no tuvieron lenguaje escrito, no fue sino hasta el siglo dieciséis que se le pudo describir. El cronista peruano, el Inca Garcilaso de la Vega—hijo de un capitán español y de una princesa incaica—escribió que el famoso Templo del Sol había sido originalmente forrado con láminas de oro e incrustado con piedras preciosas. El centenar de tumbas que yacían bajo las terrazas habían contenido las momias de las víctimas de sacrificios, así como tejidos intrincados y reliquias preciadas. Pero para la época en que la revista de la National Geographic publicó su famoso ejemplar de abril de 1913, dedicado íntegramente al hallazgo de Bingham, el lugar era esencialmente lo que vemos hoy—grande, con enigmáticas paredes de piedra y terrazas serpenteadas, oscuras estructuras de puertas y ventanas en forma de trapecio y una gran piedra pulida para ritos ceremoniales.

En verdad Bingham no había sido el primero que tropezó con Machu Picchu después de que el Inca lo dejara. Parece que a fines del siglo XIX, Augusto Berns, un aventurero alemán, escaló la montaña y saqueó el oro de la ciudadela. Los historiadores ahora indican que probablemente él llevó a Europa, ocultamente, miles de objetos para venderlos a universidades y museos, donde comenzaron a aparecer enormes cantidades de artefactos pre-Colombinos. También hay una clara evidencia

calm. The ethereal lighting, the eloquent reverence for nature, the spectacular fusion of earth and sky—these are the traveler's rewards. And, of course, these are what await you in this collection of Mike Torrey's magnificent photographs.

Here is the crest of Huayna Picchu ("Young Peak") casting a lordly shadow over the precipitous landscape. Here are the ancient aqueducts snaking artfully through walls of stone. Here is the Temple of the Sun, with its strategic apertures aligned to receive the first rays of the summer and winter solstices. Here is the Room of the Three Windows, through which we glimpse breathtaking views of mountains in the distance. Here, too, is the Intiwatana, a massive table of shiny rock that marks the sun's passage through the seasons. Here are the surrounding Andes, lost in fog or found by a dazzling sun.

In short, through Torrey's lenses, we see Machu Picchu as few mortals can. We see it at dawn. At dusk. In spring. In fall. Not once is there another human to impede us. We see its miracles through the eyes of gods.

—Marie Arana

de que eruditos nativos y habitantes de Cusco conocían la existencia de Machu Picchu antes de que Bingham lo localizara. Pero no fue sino hasta 1911 cuando uno de aquellos le indicó el trazo del camino al profesor de la Universidad de Yale, y fue entonces cuando el lugar obtuvo su renombre mundial. En el transcurso de pocos años Bingham trasladó desde Machu Picchu hasta el Museo Peabody de Yale, más de cinco mil reliquias. Más tarde, noventa y tantos años después, en el año 2007, la Universidad ha iniciado negociaciones para devolverlas.

Nada de ésto le interesa al peregrino que escala el vertiginoso camino hacia Machu Picchu. A pesar de su recargada historia, a pesar de sus esenciales misterios, el lugar todavía otorga una calma infinita. La iluminación etérea, la naturaleza que inspira un respeto elocuente, la fusión espectacular de cielo y tierra—esos son los beneficios que recibe el viajero. Y, por supuesto, es aquello lo que le aguarda en las magníficas fotografías de la colección de Mike Torrey.

Aquí está la cumbre del Huayna Picchu ("Pico Joven") repartiendo una sombra de señorío sobre el paisaje escarpado. Aquí están los antiguos acueductos atravesando las paredes de piedra, como si se tratara de diestras culebras. Aquí está el Templo del Sol con sus estratégicas aberturas en línea para recibir los primeros rayos de los solsticios de verano e invierno. Aquí está el Cuarto de las Tres Ventanas, a través de las cuales atisbamos, en la distancia, montañas que quitan el aliento. Aquí está también el Intiwatana, una enorme mesa de piedra pulida que marca el paso del Sol a través de las estaciones. Aquí están, rodeándonos, los Andes, perdidos en la niebla o hallados por un sol deslumbrante.

En resumen, a través de los lentes de Torrey, vemos Machu Picchu como pocos seres mortales lo pueden hacer. Lo vemos al amanecer. En el crepúsculo. En primavera, en otoño. Nunca más un ser human nos lo impedirá. Vemos sus milagros a través de los ojos de los dioses.

—Marie Arana

STONE OFFERINGS

Main Gate

View from lower agricultural terraces

Temple of the Sun series *(through page 43)*

Thatched roof and temple windows

First rays of sun—June Solstice

First rays of sun—December Solstice

Stairway to the rain forest

Eastern terraces and Machu Picchu Mountain

View from top of Huayna Picchu

Temple of the Condor

Artisans' Wall and Central Plaza stairway

Aqueduct series *(through page 65)*

Intiwatana series *(through page 69)*
View of Mount Yanantin

Temple of the Three Windows series *(through page 73)*

Huayna Picchu summit

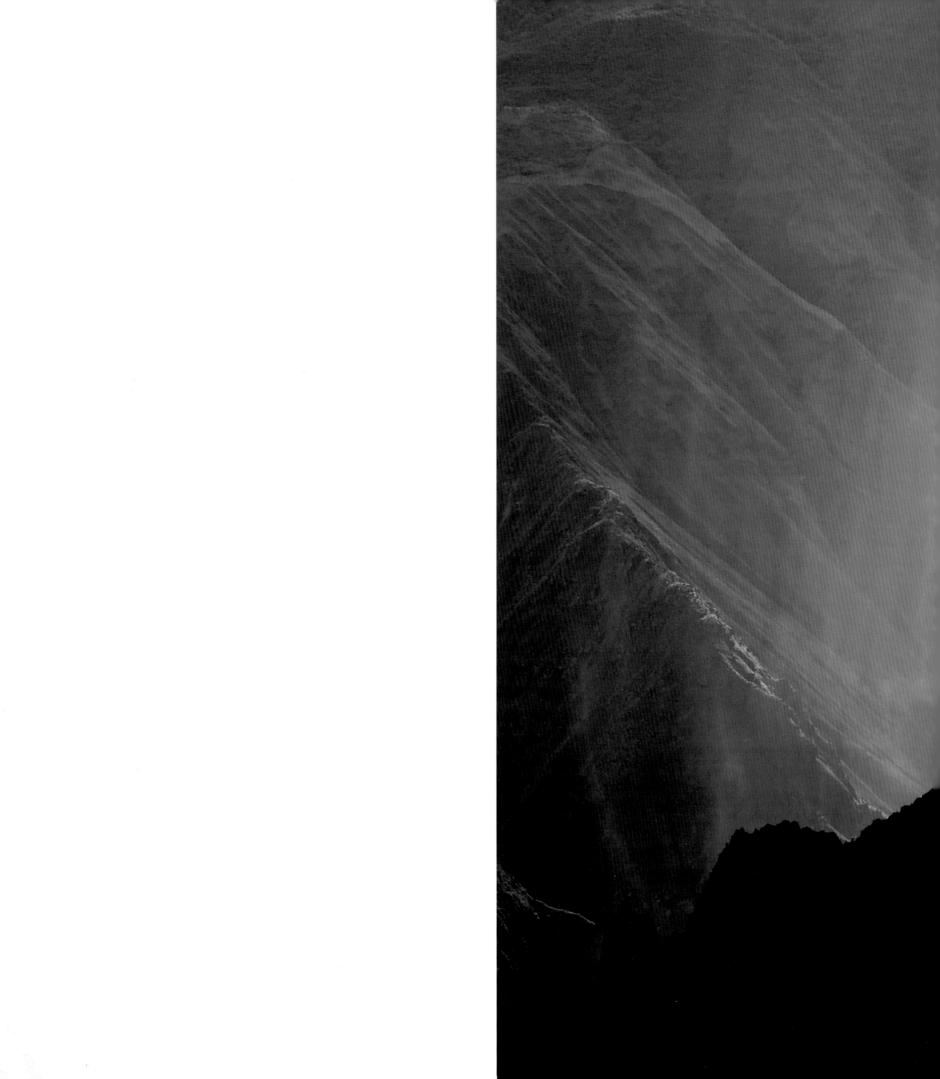

Guard House and curved upper terraces

Sacred Rock

Slide Rock

December Solstice—Inti Machay

Inside the Main Gate

Carved stone in Rock Quarry

Royal Tomb beneath Temple of the Sun

Ceremonial Rock near Guard House

Fountains and terraces

Lower agricultural terraces

Putucusi

Main Gate   Main Stairway   Sacred Plaza   Central Plaza   Aqueduct   Fountains   Slide Rock

Temple of the Three Windows   Huayna Picchu   Artisans' Wall   Temple of the Condor

Intiwatana   Temple of the Sun   Inti Machay

Rock Quarry   Uña Picchu

Looking north across Urban Sector; Agricultural Sector (not pictured) is adjacent to foreground stairway

POINTS OF INTEREST

MONUMENTS

Inti Machay: This cave on the eastern terraces has been partially enclosed by a man-made wall, creating a window that is aligned to the December Solstice.

Intiwatana: Often referred to as "Hitching Post of the Sun," this is the highest point in the Urban Sector and where important ceremonies were held. Mt. Yanantin (not pictured) in the distance is thought be part of their worship.

Royal Tomb: This cave beneath the Temple of the Sun where human remains, believed to be of royalty, were found. Beautifully carved stone makes for a remarkable entrance to this cave.

Sacred Rock: A 25-foot-long stone carved in the shape of a mountain believed to represent Machu Picchu (Ancient Peak). Positioned at the base of Huayna Picchu (Young Peak), climbers would honor the mountain prior to ascending. The back side is carved to look like an animal.

Slide Rock: Also known as "The Slide," this large rock was sheered flat at approximately a 45-degree angle. Purpose unknown.

Temple of the Condor: This monument has a carved condor head and beak on the ground paired with two wings of natural and man-made stone masses. Condors, the largest birds in the Andes, are revered by many in South America.

Temple of the Sun: A curvilinear wall of rare beauty surrounds a carved floor alter. The eastern window and alter are perfectly aligned to celebrate the first light of the June Solstice. The first light of the December Solstice is received through the temple's southern window.

Temple of the Three Windows: Also known as Room of the Three Windows. A large stone block wall framing three window openings overlooking the Central Plaza is located at the eastern edge of Sacred Plaza.

MOUNTAINS

Huayna Picchu: Meaning "Young Peak," this is the highest mountain on the north end of Machu Picchu.

Machu Picchu (not pictured): Meaning "Ancient Peak," this is the highest mountain just south of the citadel.

Putucusi (not pictured): Meaning "Happy Mountain," this lush, rounded mountain is just east of Machu Picchu.

Uña Picchu: This is the second highest mountain on the north end and adjacent to Huayna Picchu.

Mount Yanantin (not pictured): This high, pointed mountain to the east is considered very sacred.

MAJOR AREAS

The Artisans' Wall: Just off the Central Plaza at the base of the staircase, it is constructed of an uncommon salmon-colored stone.

Aqueduct: This is the source of water flowing into the fountains, brought in from the south.

Central Plaza: This is the large grassy area between the eastern and western sides of the Urban Sector.

Fountains: There are a total of 16 fountains where people could access potable water. The first is just above the Temple of the Sun, and the succession of fountains goes down the eastern terraces.

Main Gate: The only gated entry to Machu Picchu.

Rock Quarry: A major source of rocks used in the construction.

Sacred Plaza: A ceremonial area at the foot of the Intiwatana, where the Temple of the Three Windows is located.

Guard House (not pictured): This is positioned outside the Main Gate and was used in securing Machu Picchu.

AUTHOR'S NOTE

NOTA DEL AUTOR

With nearly two thousand visitors per day—more at the June and December solstices, when both my trips took place—my desire to have Machu Picchu all to myself quickly became nothing but a dream. My only option really was to photograph as if I were the only person there—to have a singular experience of Machu Picchu through the viewfinder of my camera.

In creating these images, I established a few rules to guide my process:

- Capture images without all the tourists (to whatever extent possible)
- Never ask anyone to move out of the way (the integrity of their experience was no less important than mine)
- Focus on what Machu Picchu was revealing to me

It was in narrow passages of time and space that images without people unfolded. A split second, when someone stepped behind a wall or left the frame completely, was all that I needed. At the time of the June solstice, crowds gather at the Intiwatana. While you can't see anyone in the image on page 66, if you look closely you can see the shadow of a couple who had just walked behind the magnificent carved stone they call "Hitching Post of the Sun."

For many of these images I set my camera on a tripod and then waited patiently for the light and clouds. I quickly learned that Machu Picchu would not wait for me. The environmental elements changed so rapidly that I kept my second camera ready. The image on page 72, like several others, is the only one I got before the light and clouds suddenly lost their charge.

Había un promedio de dos mil visitantes por día—un poco más en los solsticios de junio y diciembre—cuando tuvieron lugar mis viajes. Mi deseo de tener a Machu Picchu totalmente para mí de pronto se convirtió en algo así como un sueño. Mi única ilusión era, realmente, la de tomar las fotografías como si yo fuera a ser la única persona presente—tener una experiencia personal de Machu Picchu a través del visor de mi cámara. Para crear estas imágenes yo establecí unas reglas de guía para el proceso:

- *tomar imágenes sin turistas (en la medida de lo posible),*
- *nunca pedirle a nadie que se retire del sitio (la integridad de la experiencia de ellos no era inferior a la mía,*
- *y concentrarme en lo que Machu Picchu me estaba revelando.*

Fue durante cortos pasajes de tiempo y espacio que las imágenes se desarrollaban libres de visitantes. En una fracción de segundo alguien se podía deslizar detrás de una pared, o abandonar el marco completamente. Eso era todo lo que yo necesitaba. En el solsticio de junio se reunió en el Intiwatana una multitud de visitantes. En la página 66 no se ve a nadie en la imagen; mirando de cerca se puede advertir la sombra de una pareja que pasa detrás de ese calendario magníficamente cincelado en piedra al que llaman "lugar donde se amarra al Sol".

Para muchas de estas imágenes yo coloqué mi cámara fotográfica sobre un trípode y luego esperé, pacientemente, la combinación correcta de luz y nubes. Yo aprendí rápidamente que Machu Picchu no me iba a esperar. Los elementos que lo rodeaban cambiaban con tanta velocidad que yo tuve que mantener lista una segunda cámara. La imagen de la página 72, como muchas otras, es la única que tomé antes de que la luz y las nubes, súbitamente, perdieran su fuerza.

At the Temple of the Sun, it wasn't until the third and final morning that clouds finally parted, allowing the sunrise of the December Solstice to shine through the south-facing window (page 41). Unfortunately, at that moment a man stood in an out-of-bounds area directly in the frame of my camera. Knowing that this was my one remaining chance, I broke rule number two and yelled—pleaded actually—but he would not move. Nor would a passing guard intercede on my behalf. (Apparently the intruder was a government official.) So I did the next logical thing – I joined him. He continued to stand on the wall but graciously backed away so I could take this photograph.

I did not remove any people, signs, or protective barriers through retouching these images. In some you can see the top of a person's head or even a group of people in the distance. I accepted this as part the privilege to discover Machu Picchu with my own eyes.

What Machu Picchu revealed to me and I tried to capture, was that the builders of this great civilization had peeled back the canopy of a majestic rainforest and framed the implicit harmony between nature and humans. These man-made terraces expose an underlying skeleton that signifies our interconnectedness. Among these stones lies the silent offering of inspiration.

—Mike Torrey

En el Templo del Sol no fue hasta la tercera y última mañana que las nubes finalmente desaparecieron, permitiendo que el solsticio del amanecer del mes de diciembre brillara a través de la ventana que daba hacia el sur (página 41). Desgraciadamente en ese preciso instante, un individuo se detuvo en un área fuera de los límites, directamente dentro del marco de mi cámara. Sabiendo que ésta era la última oportunidad que me quedaba, rompí la regla "2" y grité—realmente yo supliqué—pero él no se iba a mover. Tampoco intercedió a mi favor un vigilante que pasaba (aparentemente el intruso era un funcionario de gobierno). Entonces tomé el siguiente paso que me dictó la lógica—me acerqué a él junto a la pared. Él continuó allí de pié, pero luego educadamente retrocedió y entonces pude tomar esta fotografía.

Yo no he borrado ni gente, ni letreros, ni barreras de protección para retocar las imágenes. En algunas fotografías se puede ver la parte alta de la cabeza de una persona, o aún se puede ver, en la distancia, a un grupo de gente. Yo lo acepté como una parte del privilegio de descubrir Machu Picchu con mis propios ojos.

Lo que Machu Picchu me reveló y lo que yo trate de lograr con mis fotografías fue la labor de los constructores de aquella época de la gran civilización Inca. Ellos habían retirado el dosel formado por una majestuosa selva tropical para darle marco a la armonía esencial que existe entre la naturaleza y la humanidad. Estas terrazas, fabricadas por el hombre, no son más que el símbolo de esa comunicación recíproca. Entre estas piedras descansa la ofrenda silenciosa de la inspiración.

—Mike Torrey

ACKNOWLEDGMENTS

The transformation of an image collection into this book could not have been rendered without the dedication, passion, and unwavering creative talent of three individuals. In producing this book, Karla Olson ensured that the bar stayed high as she expertly guided all aspects of the bookmaking process. Kirsten Rian brought a resonant artistic sensibility to the selection and sequencing of these photographs. Claudine Mansour crafted a beautiful space for revealing the inspirational qualities of this archeological wonder. To these three creative collaborators, my deepest thanks.

I am honored that Marie Arana agreed to bring her numinous voice to the book's introduction. Thanks also to Isabel Arana Cisneros of Lima, Peru, for the Spanish translation.

My thanks to Luis Vasquez of the Yantalo Peru Foundation who, on my first trip to Peru, asked if I would help his foundation raise money with my photographs of Machu Picchu. This simple question set in motion the ideas that eventually led to this book. A portion of the proceeds from *Stone Offerings* will help the Yantalo Peru Foundation build the first sustainably designed, or "green," medical clinic in South America. I encourage everyone to learn more at www.yantalo.org.

On my second trip to Peru, I encountered two acts of generosity. Erik Galindo, a photographer from Venezuela, pulled me aside to take my portrait at Machu Picchu for the simple reason that "photographers never have their portraits taken when they work—when the light is good." *Muchas gracias, mi amigo!* On Christmas Eve in Cusco, before heading home, the Salas Zapata family welcomed me into their home, where we shared dinner and I was treated to a midnight fireworks display across the entire city to celebrate the birth of *Christo. Mi más sincero agradecimiento y los mejores deseos siempre a su familia.*

I would also like to thank the following individuals for their support: Kari Rene Hall and Rick Hearn, who helped get these images ready for printing. To my friend David Marienthal, whose generosity inadvertently brought the talents of Marie Arana to my attention. To Debbie, who, when she couldn't find a coffee table book on Machu Picchu, kept encouraging me to do this one.

Interior pages printed on 157gsm NEO (FSC) matt artpaper

INDEX

WITHDRAWN